Why Little Possum's Tail Is Bare

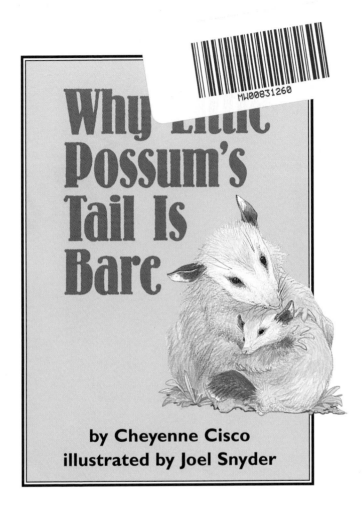

by Cheyenne Cisco
illustrated by Joel Snyder

MODERN CURRICULUM PRESS

Pearson Learning Group

Little Possum heard a buzz
He asked his mama what it was.

She said, "Bees sting!
I say so.
And that is all you have to know."

But Little Possum had to see.
Just what could that buzz-buzz be?
He had to see it, just because!
That is just the way he was.

No, Possum!

Possum did get better fast.
A little bee sting does not last.

Little Possum saw ears and a nose.
He asked his mama,
"What are those?"

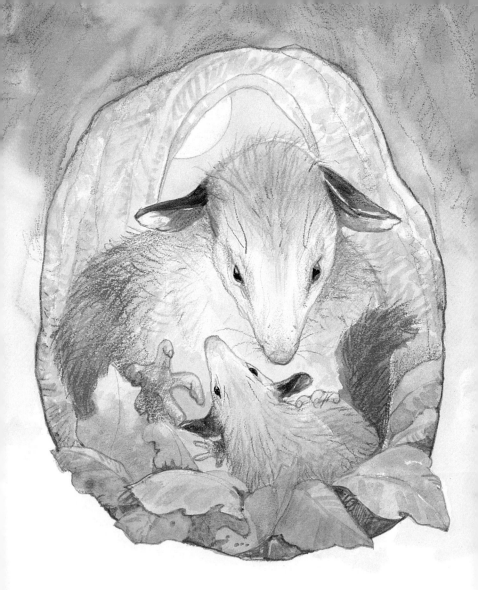

She said, "Cats nip!
I say so.
And that is all you have to know."

But Little Possum had to see.
What animal could that be?
He had to see it, just because!
That is just the way he was.

No, Possum!

Possum did get better fast.
That cat went away at last.

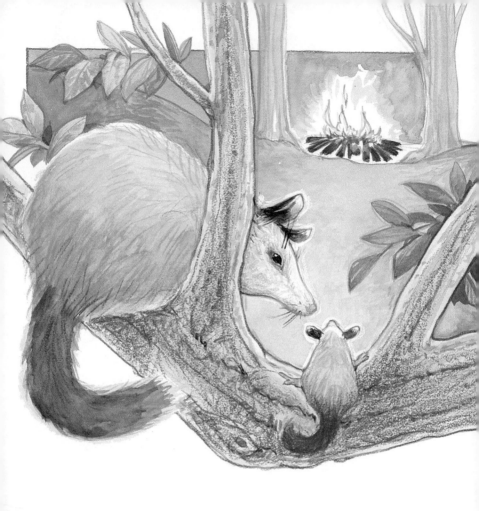

Little Possum saw a light.
He asked his mom in the night.
She said, "Fire burns!
I say so.
And that is all you have to know."

But Little Possum had to know
Just what made that hot red glow.
He had to see it, just because.
That is just the way he was.

No, Possum! No!

Little Possum did not do
what his Mama told him to.

Now all possums, here and there,
Have long tails that are quite bare.
Little Possum made it so.
And that is all you have to know!